AF444037

Table of Contents

Cinnamon Spice Red Pickles

Homemade Pickled Ginger

Pickled Asparagus

Pickled Pumpkin

Sweet Pickled Eggs

Pickled Radish and Carrots

Pickled Apples

Sweet Pickled Zucchini

Pickled Garlic

Zesty Pickled Brussels Sprouts

Pickled Corn on the Cob

Pickled Watermelon

Pickled Carrots

Spicy Pickled Malus

Pickled Sausage

Traditional Pickled Onions

Pickled Shrimp

Pickled Fish Fillet

Pickled Mostaccioli Pasta

Tangy Pickled Mushrooms

Sweet Pickled Walnuts

Pickled Squash

Pickled Pig's Feet

Pickled Bologna

Bread and Butter Pickles

Prep Time: 1 Hour

Ready In: 4 Hours 30 Minutes

Cook Time: 30 Minutes

Servings: 50

INGREDIENTS:

25 cucumbers, thinly sliced

6 onions, thinly sliced

2 green bell peppers, diced

3 cloves garlic, chopped

1/2 cup salt

3 cups cider vinegar

5 cups white sugar

2 tablespoons mustard seed

1 1/2 teaspoons celery seed

1/2 teaspoon whole cloves

1 tablespoon ground turmeric

DIRECTIONS:

1.

In a large bowl, mix together cucumbers, onions, green bell peppers, garlic and salt. Allow to stand approximately 3 hours.

2.

In a large saucepan, mix the cider vinegar, white sugar, mustard seed, celery seed, whole cloves and turmeric. Bring to a boil.

3.

Drain liquid from the cucumber mixture. Stir the mixture into the boiling vinegar mixture. Remove from heat shortly before the combined mixtures return to boil.

4.

Transfer to sterile containers. Seal and chill in the refrigerator until serving.

Pickled Jalapeno Rings

Prep Time: 5 Minutes

Ready In: 25 Minutes

Cook Time: 20 Minutes

Servings: 2

INGREDIENTS:

3/4 cup water

3/4 cup distilled white vinegar

3 tablespoons white sugar

1 tablespoon kosher salt

1 clove garlic, crushed

1/2 teaspoon oregano

10 large jalapeno peppers, sliced into rings

DIRECTIONS:

1.

Combine water, vinegar, sugar, kosher salt, garlic, and oregano in a saucepan over high heat. Bring mixture to a boil, stir in jalapeno peppers and remove from heat. Let mixture cool for 10 minutes.

2.

Pack peppers into jars using tongs, cover with vinegar mixture, cover, and refrigerate until needed.

Pickled Hot Peppers

Prep Time: 15 Minutes

Ready In: 30 Minutes

Cook Time: 15 Minutes

Servings: 40

INGREDIENTS:

1 1/2 pounds banana peppers, cut into 1 inch pieces

1 pound jalapeno peppers, cut into 1 inch pieces

1/4 pound serrano peppers, cut into 1 inch pieces

6 cups vinegar

2 cups water

3 cloves garlic, crushed

1 onion, chopped

DIRECTIONS:

1.

Place the banana peppers, jalapeno peppers, and serrano peppers into a large pot. Add the vinegar, water, garlic, and onion. Bring to a boil, then reduce heat to medium-low, and simmer for 5 minutes.

2.

Ladle peppers into sterile jars, and fill to the top with the liquid, leaving 1/4 inch headspace. Tap jars on the counter to remove air bubbles. Place two piece lids on the jars.

3.

Place jars in the rack of a large, canning pan, and fill with enough water to cover the jars completely. Bring to a boil, and boil for 10 to 15 minutes. Refrigerate jars after opening.

Pickled Southern Peaches

Prep Time: 1 Hour

Ready In: 1 Hour 25 Minutes

Cook Time: 25 Minutes

Servings: 32

INGREDIENTS:

4 cups sugar

1 cup white vinegar

1 cup water

2 tablespoons whole cloves

4 pounds fresh clingstone peaches, blanched and peeled

5 (3 inch) cinnamon sticks

DIRECTIONS:

1.

Combine the sugar, vinegar and water in a large pot, and bring to a boil. Boil for 5 minutes. Press one or two cloves into each peach, and place into the boiling syrup. Boil for 20 minutes, or until peaches are tender.

2.

Spoon peaches into sterile jars and top with liquid to 1/2 inch from the rim. Put one cinnamon stick into each jar. Wipe the rims with a clean dry cloth, and seal with lids and rings. Process in a hot water bath for 10 minutes to seal, or consult times recommended by your local extension.

Pickled Okra

Prep Time: 1 Hour

Ready In: 1 Hour

Cook Time: 1 Hour

Servings: 24

INGREDIENTS:

1 1/2 pounds fresh okra

3 dried red chile peppers

3 teaspoons dried dill

2 cups water

1 cup vinegar

  2 tablespoons salt

DIRECTIONS:

1.

Divide the fresh okra evenly between 3 sterile (1 pint) jars. Place one dried chile, and one teaspoon of dill into each jar.

2.

In a small saucepan, combine the water, vinegar and salt. Bring to a rolling boil. Pour over the ingredients in the jars, and seal in a hot water bath for 10 minutes. Refrigerate jars after opening.

Crispy Pickled Green Beans

Prep Time: 1 Hour

Ready In: 1 Hour 10 Minutes

Cook Time: 10 Minutes

Servings: 48

INGREDIENTS:

2 1/2 pounds fresh green beans

2 1/2 cups distilled white vinegar

2 cups water

1/4 cup salt

1 clove garlic, peeled

1 bunch fresh dill weed

  3/4 teaspoon red pepper flakes (optional)

DIRECTIONS:

1.

Sterilize 6 (1/2 pint) jars with rings and lids and keep hot. Trim green beans to 1/4 inch shorter than your jars.

2.

In a large saucepan, stir together the vinegar, water and salt. Add garlic and bring to a rolling boil over high heat. In each jar, place 1 sprig of dill and 1/8 teaspoon of red pepper flakes. Pack green beans into the jars so they are standing on their ends.

3.

Ladle the boiling brine into the jars, filling to within 1/4 inch of the tops. Discard garlic. Seal jars with lids and rings. Place in a hot water bath so they are covered by 1 inch of water. Simmer but do not boil for 10 minutes to process. Cool to room temperature. Test jars for a good seal by pressing on the center of the lid. It should not move. Refrigerate any jars that do not seal properly. Let pickles ferment for 2 to 3 weeks before eating.

Sweet Pickled Blueberries

Prep Time: 5 Minutes

Ready In: 8 Hours 40 Minutes

Cook Time: 35 Minutes

Servings: 96

INGREDIENTS:

3 (3 inch) cinnamon sticks

1 teaspoon whole cloves

1 teaspoon whole allspice berries

1 1/2 cups red wine vinegar

2 quarts fresh blueberries, washed and picked over

1 cup white sugar

1 cup brown sugar

1.

Place the cinnamon sticks, cloves, and allspice berries onto the center of a 8 inch square piece of cheesecloth. Gather together the edges of the cheesecloth, and tie with kitchen twine to secure. Place spice sachet into a large saucepan and pour in the vinegar. Bring to a simmer over medium heat; cook for 5 minutes. Stir blueberries into the vinegar; cook until heated through, about 5 minutes. As the blueberries heat, gently shake the pot. Do not stir to avoid breaking the berries. Remove from heat, cover, and let stand at room temperature for 8 to 12 hours.

2.

Pour berries and liquid into a colander set over a bowl. Remove spice sachet. Transfer berries to hot, sterilized canning jars; reserve the liquid. Return liquid to saucepan and place over high heat. Stir in the white and brown sugars; bring to a boil. Boil until thickened, about 4 minutes. Ladle hot syrup over berries, leaving 1/2 inch headspace. Wipe the rims of the jars with a moist paper towel to remove any food residue. Top with sterilized lids; screw on rings.

3.

Place a rack in the bottom of a large stockpot and fill halfway with water. Bring to a boil over high heat, then carefully lower the jars into the pot. Leave a 2 inch space between the jars. Pour in more boiling water if necessary until the water level is at least 1 inch above the tops of the jars. Bring the water to a full boil, cover the pot, and process for 15 minutes.

Cinnamon Spice Red Pickles

Prep Time: 40 Minutes

Ready In: 1 Day 15 Hours 5 Minutes

Cook Time: 2 Hours 25 Minutes

Servings: 80

INGREDIENTS:

7 pounds large cucumbers

1 cup pickling lime (calcium hydroxide)

2 teaspoons red food coloring

1 teaspoon powdered alum

1 cup distilled white vinegar

7 cups white sugar

2 cups distilled white vinegar

2 cups water

1 cup cinnamon red hot candies

  4 cinnamon sticks

DIRECTIONS:

1.

Peel cucumbers, halve lengthwise, and scrape out the seeds with a spoon. Cut the cucumber into 1/4 inch half circles, and place into a glass or ceramic crock. Dissolve the pickling lime in about 1 quart of room temperature water, pour over the cucumbers, then add additional water until the cucumbers are covered by 1/2 inch. Let stand at room temperature 24 hours.

2.

Drain the cucumbers and rinse well with cold water. Place into a large stockpot, and cover with cold water. Allow to stand for 3 hours, then drain and rinse again. Return the cucumbers to the pot, add the food coloring, alum, 1 cup vinegar, and enough water to cover by 1/2 inch. Bring to a boil over high heat, then reduce heat to a simmer, and cook 2 hours. Once the cucumbers have cooked for 2 hours, drain and allow to cool a bit before placing into the glass or ceramic jar.

3.

Stir together sugar, 2 cups vinegar, 2 cups water, cinnamon red hot candies, and cinnamon sticks in a saucepan over medium heat until the sugar and candies dissolve. Pour this mixture over the warm cucumbers, cover, and let stand overnight. Pack pickles into pint jars, and process in

a hot water bath for 15 to 20 minutes. Refrigerate any jars that do not
seal.

Homemade Pickled Ginger

Prep Time: 40 Minutes

Ready In: 45 Minutes

Cook Time: 5 Minutes

Servings: 32

INGREDIENTS:

8 ounces fresh young ginger root, peeled

1 1/2 teaspoons sea salt

1 cup rice vinegar

  1/3 cup white sugar

DIRECTIONS:

1.

Cut the ginger into chunks and place them into a bowl. Sprinkle with sea
salt, stir to coat and let stand for about 30 minutes. Transfer the ginger
to a clean jar.

2.

In a saucepan, stir together the rice vinegar and sugar until sugar has
dissolved. Bring to a boil, then pour the boiling liquid over the ginger
root pieces in the jar.

3.

Allow the mixture to cool, then put the lid on the jar and store in the
refrigerator for at least one week. You will see that the liquid will change
to slightly pinkish in few minutes. Don't be alarmed because it's the
reaction of rice vinegar that causes the change. Only quality rice vinegar
can do that! Some commercial pickled ginger has red coloring added.
Cut pieces of ginger into paper thin slices for serving.

Pickled Asparagus

Prep Time: 40 Minutes

Ready In: 45 Minutes

Cook Time: 5 Minutes

Servings: 32

INGREDIENTS:

30 asparagus spears

1/3 cup coarse salt

2 quarts cold water

1 2/3 cups distilled white vinegar

2/3 cup sugar

1 teaspoon coarse salt

1 teaspoon mustard seed

1 1/2 teaspoons dill seed

1 white onion, sliced into rings

1/2 teaspoon chili pepper flakes

2 sprigs fresh dill

DIRECTIONS:

1.

Trim the cut end of the asparagus spears, and cut them into 3 inch lengths. Place them in a large bowl with 1/3 cup salt, and cover with water. Let stand for 2 hours. Drain and rinse under cool water, and pat dry.

2.

Sterilize two pint size wide mouth jars in simmering water for 5 minutes. In a saucepan over medium heat, combine the vinegar, sugar, 1 teaspoon of salt, mustard seed, dill seed and onion rings. Bring to a boil, and boil for one minute.

3.

Pack the asparagus spears, tips up, in the hot jars leaving 1/2 of space
from the rim. Tuck one dill sprig into each jar, and sprinkle in 1/4
teaspoon of red pepper flakes. Pour hot pickling liquid into the jars,
filling to within 1/4 inch of the rim. Wipe rims with a clean damp cloth,
and seal with lids. Process in a boiling water bath for 10 minutes. Cool to
room temperature. Check seals when cool by pressing the center of the
lid. It should not move. Label and date; store in a cool dark place. If any
jars have not sealed properly, refrigerate and eat within two weeks.

Pickled Pumpkin

Prep Time: 13 Hours 50 Minutes

Ready In: 14 Hours 5 Minutes

Cook Time: 15 Minutes

Servings: 32

INGREDIENTS:

4 pounds peeled and diced pumpkin

5 cups white sugar

5 cups distilled white vinegar

4 cinnamon sticks

15 whole cloves

DIRECTIONS:

1.

Place the pumpkin in a large, deep bowl.

2.

In a large saucepan, mix the sugar, vinegar, cinnamon sticks and cloves.
Boil 5 minutes. Pour the hot liquid over the pumpkin in the bowl. Cover
and set aside 8 hours, or overnight.

3.

Strain the liquid into a large saucepan. Boil 5 minutes. Remove the cinnamon sticks and cloves, leaving a few bits for decoration. Place the pumpkin back into the liquid and return to boiling. Boil 5 minutes, or until pumpkin is transparent but crisp. Allow the mixture to cool. Transfer to sterile jars and refrigerate.

Sweet Pickled Eggs

Prep Time: 13 Hours 50 Minutes

Ready In: 14 Hours 5 Minutes

Cook Time: 15 Minutes

Servings: 32

INGREDIENTS:

12 eggs

1 large onion, sliced into rings

2 cups white wine vinegar

2 cups water

1/2 cup white sugar

1 teaspoon salt

1 tablespoon pickling spice, wrapped in cheesecloth

DIRECTIONS:

1.

Cover eggs with water in a large pot. Cover with lid. Bring to a boil over medium-high heat. Boil gently for 10 minutes. Drain. Run cold water over eggs until they are cold. Shell eggs.

2.

Prepare the brine in a sauce pan by combining the vinegar, water, sugar and salt. Stir over medium heat until sugar is dissolved.

3.

Layer the eggs (whole) and onion rings in a sterilized 2 quart jar to within 1 inch of the top.

4.

Add pickling spice to brine. Swirl bag around for 30 seconds. Remove bag. Pour brine over eggs to fill jar with 1/4 inch from top. Seal with a sterilized lid. Store in the refrigerator for 1 to 2 weeks before serving. Serve chilled.

Pickled Radish and Carrots

Prep Time: 20 Minutes

Ready In: 5 Hours 20 Minutes

Cook Time: 20 Minutes

Servings: 4

INGREDIENTS:

1/2 cup distilled white vinegar

1/4 cup white sugar

1 small carrot, peeled and cut into matchsticks

1 daikon radish, peeled and cut into matchsticks

2 tablespoons chopped fresh cilantro

1 Thai chile pepper, seeded and chopped

DIRECTIONS:

1.

Heat vinegar and sugar in a saucepan over low heat until sugar is dissolved. Remove from heat, and refrigerate to cool. Place daikon and carrot in a glass jar with the cilantro and chile peppers. Pour the cooled vinegar mixture over, submerging the vegetables. Cover and refrigerate for at least 4 hours, or overnight.

Pickled Apples

Prep Time: 20 Minutes
Ready In: 2 Hours 22 Minutes
Cook Time: 2 Minutes
Servings: 16

INGREDIENTS:

1 cup water

1 cup cider vinegar

1 cup white sugar

1 tablespoon whole allspice berries

1 tablespoon whole cloves

1 tablespoon ground nutmeg

1 tablespoon ground ginger

6 apples - peeled, cored and sliced

1/2 cup lemon juice

DIRECTIONS:

1.

Place the water, cider vinegar, sugar, allspice, clove, nutmeg, and ginger into a small saucepan, and bring to a simmer over medium-high heat, stirring until the sugar dissolves.

2.

Meanwhile, toss the sliced apples with the lemon juice, and pack into two sterilized 1 quart canning jars with lids and rings. Pour the boiling syrup over the apples, and affix the lids and rings.

3.

Allow the jars to stand at room temperature until cool. Once cool, press the top of each lid with a finger, ensuring that the seal is tight (lid does not move up or down at all). Place in the refrigerator, and wait 1 week before opening.

Sweet Pickled Zucchini

Prep Time: 2 Days 3 Hours 30 Minutes
Ready In: 2 Days 4 Hours 15 Minutes
Cook Time: 45 Minutes
Servings: 50

INGREDIENTS:

1 gallon water

16 cups peeled and cubed zucchini

1 cup pickling lime (calcium hydroxide)

1 gallon water

2 cups apple cider vinegar

8 cups white sugar

3 teaspoons pickling spice

2 teaspoons salt

DIRECTIONS:

1.

Place the zucchini into one gallon water in a large bowl. Stir in the pickling lime, and let stand for 24 hours. Drain and rinse the zucchini a few times, then cover with a fresh gallon water. Let stand for 3 hours, then drain.

2.

Heat the vinegar, sugar, pickling spice, and salt in a large pot over medium heat until the sugar dissolves. Stir in the drained zucchini. Cover and rest the zucchini for 24 hours. Bring the zucchini mixture to a simmer over medium heat for 35 minutes. Allow to cool.

3.

Sterilize about 10 pint-sized jars and lids in boiling water for at least 5 minutes. Divide and pack the zucchini mixture evenly into the hot, sterilized jars, filling the jars to within 1/4 inch of the top. Run a knife or a thin spatula around the insides of the jars after they have been filled to remove any air bubbles. Wipe the rims of the jars with a moist paper towel to remove any food residue. Top with lids, and screw on rings. Store in the refrigerator.

Pickled Garlic

Cook Time: 10 Minutes

Ready In: 10 Minutes

Cook Time: 10 Minutes

Servings: 6

INGREDIENTS:

6 bulbs garlic

4 cups white wine vinegar

1/4 cup white sugar

1 teaspoon whole black peppercorns

4 whole cloves

1 bay leaf

2 dried red chile peppers

1 1/2 tablespoons lemon zest

DIRECTIONS:

1.

Trim the tops from the heads of garlic. Peel off all but one layer of the outer skin. Set aside.

2.

In a saucepan, combine the vinegar, sugar, peppercorns, cloves, bay leaf, chile peppers and lemon zest. Bring to a boil and cook for 2 minutes. Add the garlic, and continue to boil for another 4 minutes. Remove from the heat and let stand overnight at room temperature.

3.

Transfer to a clean jar. Strain the brine into the jar with the garlic so that the heads are completely covered. Discard the solids. Cover and store in the refrigerator until using. It will keep for 6 to 8 weeks. To keep longer, store in sterile jars and process in a hot water bath for at least 10 minutes to seal the jars.

Zesty Pickled Brussels Sprouts

Prep Time: 20 Minutes

Ready In: 21 Days 40 Minutes

Cook Time: 20 Minutes

Servings: 40

INGREDIENTS:

2 pounds Brussels sprouts, trimmed and cut in half

5 1-pint canning jars with lids and rings

5 cloves garlic, divided

1 1/4 teaspoons red pepper flakes, divided

5 cups water

5 cups distilled white vinegar

7 tablespoons pickling salt

DIRECTIONS:

1.   Soak Brussels sprouts in a large bowl filled with lightly salted water for about 15 minutes. Drain well. Sterilize the jars and lids in boiling water for at least 5 minutes. Divide the drained Brussels sprouts evenly between jars, filling the jars about 3/4-inch from the top. Place 1 garlic clove and 1/4 teaspoon red pepper flakes in each jar.

2.   Bring vinegar, water, and pickling salt to a boil in a large pot over medium-high heat until the salt is dissolved, about 5 minutes. Pour the vinegar mixture into the jars, filling the jars to within 1/4 inch of the to. Run a knife or a thin spatula around the insides of the jars after they have been filled to remove any air bubbles. Wipe the rims of the jars

with a moist paper towel to remove any food residue. Top with lids, and screw on rings.

3.

Place a rack in the bottom of a large stockpot, and fill stockpot halfway with water. Bring to a boil over high heat, then carefully lower the jars into the pot using a holder. Leave a 2-inch space between the jars. Pour in more boiling water if necessary, until the water level is at least 1 inch above the tops of the jars. Bring the water to a full boil, cover the pot, and process for 10 minutes. Remove the jars from the stockpot and place onto a cloth-covered or wood surface, several inches apart, until cool. Once cool, press the top of each lid with a finger, ensuring that the seal is tight (lid does not move up or down at all). Store in a cool, dark area, and wait at least 3 weeks before opening.

Pickled Corn on the Cob

Prep Time: 15 Minutes

Ready In: 30 Minutes

Cook Time: 15 Minutes

Servings: 12

INGREDIENTS:

6 ears corn - husked, cleaned and quartered

1 tablespoon salt

3 cups white vinegar

1 cup white sugar

1 tablespoon pickling spice

2 bay leaves

1 (3 inch) cinnamon stick

DIRECTIONS:

1.

Rinse the corn, and place in a large bowl with the salt and enough water to cover. Refrigerate until needed. Sterilize two 1quart jars in simmering water for 5 minutes. In a large stock pot, stir together the vinegar, sugar and pickling spice. Add the bay leaves and cinnamon stick. Bring to a boil over medium heat, stirring occasionally to be sure the sugar has dissolved.

2.

Drain and rinse the corn under cold water. Add to the pot with the pickling mixture. Return to a boil, reduce heat to low, and simmer for 10 minutes. Remove corn with a slotted spoon, and fill the sterile jars. Remove the cinnamon stick and bay leaves from the liquid, and discard. Fill the jars of corn with the vinegar mixture to within 1/2 inch of the top. The corn should be completely covered. Wipe the rims of the jars with a clean cloth. Seal with lids and rings.

3.

Process the jars in a hot water bath for the time recommended by your local extension in your area. Most areas require about 10 minutes in a water bath of 180 degrees F (82 degrees C). Refrigerate after opening.

Pickled Watermelon

Prep Time: 45 Minutes

Ready In: 9 Hours 35 Minutes

Cook Time: 50 Minutes

Servings: 18

INGREDIENTS:

1/4 cup salt

2 pounds watermelon rind, white part only, cut into 1-inch cubes

4 cups white sugar

2 cups white vinegar

2 cups water

1 lemon, thinly sliced

2 tablespoons broken cinnamon stick

1 tablespoon whole cloves

1 18-inch square of cheesecloth

3 (1 pint) canning jars with lids and rings

DIRECTIONS:

1.

Dissolve salt in a large bowl with enough water to cover the trimmed watermelon rind cubes (all green and red parts removed). Soak the watermelon rind overnight in the salty water. Drain, rinse, and place the rind cubes into a large saucepan over medium heat. Bring to a boil, reduce heat to a simmer, and cook until tender, about 10 minutes. Drain the rind in a colander set in the sink.

2.

Mix the sugar, vinegar, and 2 cups of water in a large bowl, stirring until the sugar has dissolved. Place the lemon, cinnamon, and cloves into a a piece of cheesecloth, and tie the corners together to make a spice bag. Place the spice bag into the pot, and stir in the watermelon rind pieces. Bring to a boil, reduce heat to a simmer, and cook until the watermelon rind becomes translucent, about 35 minutes. Remove the spice bag.

3.

Sterilize the jars and lids in boiling water for at least 5 minutes. Pack the watermelon pickle into the hot, sterilized jars, filling the jars to within 1/4 inch of the top. Run a knife or a thin spatula around the insides of the jars after they have been filled to remove any air bubbles. Wipe the rims of the jars with a moist paper towel to remove any food residue. Top with lids, and screw on rings.

4.

Place a rack in the bottom of a large stockpot and fill halfway with water. Bring to a boil over high heat, then carefully lower the jars into the pot using a holder. Leave a 2 inch space between the jars. Pour in more boiling water if necessary until the water level is at least 1 inch above the tops of the jars. Bring the water to a full boil, cover the pot, and process for 10 minutes, or the time recommended for your area.

5.

Remove the jars from the stockpot and place onto a cloth-covered or

wood surface, several inches apart, until cool. Once cool, press the top of
each lid with a finger, ensuring that the seal is tight (lid does not move up
or down at all).

Pickled Carrots

Prep Time: 10 Minutes

Ready In: 12 Hours 25 Minutes

Cook Time: 15 Minutes

Servings: 32

INGREDIENTS:

1 cup distilled white vinegar

2 tablespoons white sugar

1 teaspoon salt

1/8 teaspoon ground black pepper

2/3 cup water

  8 large carrots, diced

DIRECTIONS:

1.

In a medium saucepan, mix distilled white vinegar, white sugar, salt,
pepper and water. Bring the mixture to a boil. Remove from heat and
allow to cool slightly.

2.

Place the carrots in sterile containers. Cover with the vinegar solution.
Seal the containers, refrigerate and marinate carrots 12 hours or
overnight before serving.

Spicy Pickled Malus

Prep Time: 30 Minutes
Ready In: 50 Minutes
Cook Time: 20 Minutes
Servings: 24

INGREDIENTS:

6 quarts fresh crabapples, washed and stems removed

1 cup whole cloves

1/2 cup water

3 pounds brown sugar

1 cup distilled white vinegar

2 tablespoons whole allspice berries

6 cinnamon sticks

1 tablespoon grated lemon zest

DIRECTIONS:

1.

Stick 2 or 3 cloves into each of the crabapples, and set aside.

2.

In a large pot, stir together the water, sugar, and vinegar. Place allspice berries, cinnamon sticks, and lemon zest in cheesecloth, and tie cheesecloth to make a small bag; add to pot. Bring to a boil, then reduce heat and simmer for 5 minutes. Add the crabapples,and simmer until tender, about 20 minutes.

3.

Use a slotted spoon to lift out crabapples and place them into sterile jars. Cover with hot syrup, and seal in a hot water bath for 10 minutes, or until the centers of the lids are depressed. If the syrup seems too thick, add more water. Refrigerate after opening.

Pickled Sausage

Prep Time: 5 Minutes

Cook Time: 5 Minutes

Ready In: 10 Minutes

Servings: 10

INGREDIENTS:

4 cups water

2 tablespoons salt

4 cups distilled white vinegar

10 drops red food coloring (optional)

  10 links smoked beef sausage

DIRECTIONS:

1.

In a large pot over medium-high heat, combine the water, salt, vinegar, and red food coloring. Bring to a boil. Cut the sausage links into halves or thirds, depending on size, and place into a large sterile jar. Pour the hot vinegar mixture in with the sausage, secure the lid, and let stand for 2 days before serving.

Traditional Pickled Onions

Prep Time: 25 Minutes

Cook Time: 10 Minutes

Ready In: 1 Day 35 Minutes

Servings: 32

INGREDIENTS:

2 1/4 pounds pearl onions, peeled

1/2 cup salt

3 cups malt vinegar

1 tablespoon mixed pickling spice

2 dried chile peppers, crumbled (optional)

1 clove garlic, crushed

   2 bay leaves

DIRECTIONS:

1.

Place the peeled onions in a glass or ceramic bowl and cover with cold water. Drain the water into a saucepan and stir in the salt. Bring just to a boil so that the salt dissolves, then cool slightly and pour over the onions. Cover the bowl with a heavy plate so all of the onions stay submerged. Leave onions to stand for 24 hours.

2.

Measure the vinegar into a saucepan. Tie the pickling spice into a cloth and add to the vinegar along with the bay leaves. Bring to a boil, then simmer over low heat for 5 minutes.

3.

Rinse the onions and pat them dry. Add to the saucepan with the vinegar. Simmer for 2 to 3 minutes. Pack the onions into sterile jars and ladle the brine over them until they are covered. Add a dried chile pepper to each jar if you like. Seal with sterile lids and rings and store in a cool dark place for at least 6 weeks before opening.

Pickled Shrimp

Prep Time: 20 Minutes

Ready In: 25 Minutes

Cook Time: 5 Minutes

Servings: 12

INGREDIENTS:

3 pounds large shrimp - peeled and deveined

1 large onion, thinly sliced

1 green bell pepper, cut into thin strips

1 cup vegetable oil

2 cups ketchup

1 cup apple cider vinegar

2 tablespoons white sugar

2 (8 ounce) jars prepared yellow mustard

2 tablespoons capers

1 teaspoon garlic powder

2 tablespoons Worcestershire sauce

1 teaspoon salt

1 teaspoon ground black pepper

2 dashes hot pepper sauce

DIRECTIONS:

1.

Bring a large pot of lightly salted water to a boil. Add shrimp, and cook for about 5 minutes, until pink. Drain and set aside.

2.

Place the onion and green pepper in a large bowl. Add vegetable oil, ketchup, cider vinegar, sugar, mustard, and capers. Season with garlic powder, Worcestershire sauce, salt, pepper and hot sauce, and mix until well blended. Place shrimp into the bowl with the sauce, cover, and refrigerate until thoroughly chilled. Serve cold.

Pickled Fish Fillet

Prep Time: 30 Minutes

Ready In: 30 Minutes

Cook Time: 1 Hour

Servings: 6

INGREDIENTS:

1/2 cup vegetable oil for frying

3 pounds cod fillets, cut into 2 to 3 ounce portions

salt to taste

2 large onions, peeled and sliced into rings

2 cloves garlic, chopped

8 whole black peppercorns

4 whole allspice berries

3 bay leaves

1 red chile pepper, seeded and sliced lengthwise

2 cups red wine vinegar

1/2 cup water

1/2 cup packed brown sugar, or to taste

2 tablespoons curry powder

1 teaspoon ground turmeric

2 teaspoons ground cumin

2 teaspoons ground coriander

DIRECTIONS:

1.

Heat the oil in a large skillet over medium-high heat. Season the fish with salt and place in the skillet. Fry on both sides until fish is browned and cooked through, about 5 minutes per side. Remove from the skillet and set aside.

2.

Fry the onions and garlic in the same skillet over medium heat until translucent. Add the peppercorns, allspice berries, bay leaves, and red chile pepper. Pour in the vinegar and water and bring to a boil. Stir in the brown sugar until dissolved. Season with curry powder, turmeric, cumin and coriander. Taste and adjust the sweetness if desired. Layer pieces of fish and the pickling mixture in a serving dish. Pour the liquid over until the top layer is covered. Allow to cool then cover and refrigerate for at least 24 hours before serving.

Pickled Mostaccioli Pasta

Prep Time: 30 Minutes

Ready In: 40 Minutes

Cook Time: 10 Minutes

Servings: 12

INGREDIENTS:

1 (16 ounce) package mostaccioli pasta

1 1/2 cups white vinegar

1 1/2 cups white sugar

2 tablespoons prepared yellow mustard

1 teaspoon garlic powder

1 teaspoon salt

1 teaspoon ground black pepper

1 teaspoon dried parsley

1 medium onion, quartered

1 medium cucumber, diced

DIRECTIONS:

1.

Bring a large pot of lightly salted water to a boil. Add the pasta, and cook for 8 to 10 minutes, until tender. Drain and cool, then transfer to a large bowl.

2.

In a blender or large food processor, combine the vinegar, sugar, mustard, garlic powder, salt, pepper, parsley, onion and cucumber. Puree until it forms a smooth sauce, about 3 minutes.

3.

Pour over the pasta, and stir to coat evenly. Cover, and refrigerate for 3 days before serving. Stir once a day.

Tangy Pickled Mushrooms

Prep Time: 20 Minutes
Ready In: 40 Minutes
Cook Time: 20 Minutes
Servings: 8

INGREDIENTS:

1 1/2 pounds fresh mushrooms

1 1/2 ounces fresh ginger root

1 lemon peel, cut into strips

1 onion, thinly sliced

4 cups white wine vinegar

3 teaspoons sea salt

1 teaspoon black peppercorns

DIRECTIONS:

1.

Wipe the mushrooms with a damp cloth to clean them, and trim the stalks so that they are even with the caps. Place mushrooms in a medium saucepan.

2.

Peel the ginger and cut into quarters. Add to the mushrooms, along with the lemon zest, onion, vinegar, salt and peppercorns. Bring the mixture to a boil and simmer for 15-20 minutes, or until mushrooms are tender.

3.

Remove the mushrooms from the cooking liquid with a slotted spoon and pack into sterilized jars. Strain the cooking liquid and bring it back to a boil. Pour hot liquid over the mushrooms until the level of the liquid is 1/2 inch above the mushrooms. Seal the jars and store in the refrigerator.

Sweet Pickled Walnuts

Prep Time: 20 Minutes

Ready In: 40 Minutes

Cook Time: 20 Minutes

Servings: 32

INGREDIENTS:

4 pounds fresh young black walnuts (in shell)

3/4 cup salt

4 cups malt vinegar

2 1/8 cups packed brown sugar

1 teaspoon ground allspice

1 teaspoon ground cloves

1/2 teaspoon ground cinnamon

1 tablespoon grated fresh ginger root

DIRECTIONS:

1.

Use rubber gloves to handle the young walnuts and pierce each one a few times with the tines of a fork. Watch out for the clear juice this produces. It stains a dark, espresso brown and is a natural dye. Place the walnuts into a bucket and fill with enough water to cover. Stir in 3/4 cup of salt to make a brine. Soak walnuts for 1 week, then drain and make the brine again. Soak for 1 more week.

2.

After the second week, drain the walnuts and lay them out on trays to dry in an airy place. In a couple of days they will turn black. Once they have all turned black, they are ready to pickle. In a large pot, stir together the malt vinegar, brown sugar, allspice, cloves, cinnamon and ginger. Bring to a boil and then add the walnuts. Simmer over medium heat for 15 minutes. Remove from heat and allow to cool.

3.

Spoon the walnuts into sterile jars and fill with the syrup to within 1/2 inch of the top. Seal with lids and rings. Store in the refrigerator or process in a hot water bath for 10 minutes. Cool to room temperature and store in a cool dark place.

Pickled Squash

Prep Time: 4 Hours

Ready In: 4 Hours 5 Minutes

Cook Time: 5 Minutes

Servings: 4

INGREDIENTS:

1/4 cup salt

2 1/2 pounds young yellow squash and zucchini, sliced into rounds

1 green bell pepper, seeded and sliced into strips

2 small onions, thinly sliced

2 1/4 cups white sugar

2 cups distilled white vinegar

2 teaspoons mustard seed

1 teaspoon ground turmeric

1 teaspoon celery seed

DIRECTIONS:

1.

In a large non-aluminum pot, combine the squash, bell pepper, and onions. Cover with salt, and let stand for 2 hours to release the liquids. Stir occasionally.

2.

Just before the 2 hours are up, combine the sugar, vinegar, mustard seed, turmeric and celery seed in a saucepan. Bring to a boil. Drain the salty liquid from the vegetables. Pour the spice brine over the vegetables, and let stand for 2 more hours.

3.

Bring to a boil once again, and simmer for about 5 minutes. Ladle into 1 pint sterile jars, filling with the liquid to within 1/4 inch of the top. Wipe rims with a clean towel, and run a thin spatula around the inside of the jar to remove air bubbles. Seal with lids and rings. Process for 10 minutes in a simmering water bath to seal completely.

Pickled Pig's Feet

Prep Time: 25 Minutes

Ready In: 14 Hours 25 Minutes

Cook Time: 1 Hour

Servings: 8

INGREDIENTS:

5 pig's feet

1 small ham hock

2 bay leaves

3 teaspoons salt

3 dried red chile pepper

1 large onion, chopped

  2 cups white vinegar, or to taste

DIRECTIONS:

1.

Place the pig's feet in a large pot with the ham hock, bay leaves, salt, chile peppers, and onion. Cover with cold water. Bring to a boil, reduce heat, and simmer 1 hour, or until meat is easily removed from the bone. Remove from heat, and set aside to cool.

2.

Remove pieces of pork from the liquid, reserving liquid in a separate container. Remove skin and most of the fat from the pork. Separate feet into pieces, and remove the meat from the ham hock. Discard ham hock bone, fat, and skin.

3.

Place the feet and meaty bits in a 1-quart jar with a lid. Strain the liquid, and pour over meat, leaving room for the vinegar. Stir in the vinegar. Seal jar, and let stand in refrigerator overnight. Skim off the cooled layer of fat from the top before eating.

Pickled Bologna

Prep Time: 20 Minutes

Ready In: 30 Minutes

Cook Time: 10 Minutes

Servings: 10

INGREDIENTS:

2 pounds ring bologna, peeled and sliced into large chunks

4 cups vinegar

1 (4.5 ounce) can chopped pickled jalapeno peppers

1 onion, chopped

1 cup water

1 tablespoon hot pepper sauce

1 tablespoon salt

DIRECTIONS:

1.

Place the bologna in a large sealable jar. Combine the vinegar, peppers, onion, water, hot pepper sauce, and salt in a saucepan; bring to a boil; pour over the bologna. Seal the jar. Shake daily. Allow to pickle at least 3 days. For best results, allow bologna to pickle 90 days.

www.ingramcontent.com/pod-product-compliance
Lightning Source LLC
Chambersburg PA
CBHW020136180726
47992CB00023B/3207